The Journey
Night to Dawn

Laila Sahar Jewayni

DEDICATION

This book is dedicated to Afghanistan—to my ancestors who live in my bones. To my parents who gave me everything they had and more. It's dedicated to the beautiful mystery of life, and most of all, to the journey.

The Journey: Night to Dawn

.

"MUSIC GIVES A SOUL TO THE
UNIVERSE, WINGS TO THE MIND,
FLIGHT TO THE IMAGINATION, AND
LIFE TO EVERYTHING."

– PLATO

For your listening pleasure, go to your Spotify app +
press the search button, at the top right click on the
camera icon + scan the code. Light a candle or incense
+ press play!

The Journey: Night to Dawn

WELCOME

Thank you for taking the time to go on this journey with me. I hope you will read these pages with an open heart. The words that I have written here are the most vulnerable parts of me. For a long time, I kept these words to myself, and today I am sharing them with you. They come from my own lived experience and what I have seen around me. Held in these words are some of my darkest times and my most bright. May you find something in here that speaks to your soul.

The Journey: Night to Dawn

LAILA ("NIGHT")

They call me night,
like the night moon
I will illuminate
your darkness.

They call me night,
never afraid to
dim the world
for it is the
only way
to see the light.

They call me night,
let me be your refuge
when the day
refuses to set
you free.

And when the
black cape covers
the sky,
lay your head
on my pillow
and call me
night.

There's a
sweetness
to us
that smells
of lifetimes.

PURITY

There is that
touch that
I want.

That touch
that I want
on the curve
of my hip,
on the corner
of my lip,
that sweet
tenderness
that's so soft
it almost
doesn't exist.

LETTER TO MY BELOVED

You make me feel like
time stands still and
centuries have passed
when our eyes meet.

And when our eyes meet,
I feel the warmth of
your smile wrapping itself
around my wounds.

I feel my body tingling
with desire
and every glance,
blazes the fire inside.

You make me feel like
every inch of my body
exudes unconditional love.

You make me feel like
I'm home at last
even when lost.

You make me feel like
the future of the world
depends on me.

A world plagued with
uncertainty somehow

becomes certain,
when you make me feel—
because you—
make me feel good.

Like so good
that I can conquer my fears
and wipe away my tears
and just live in my very
pureness.
To harness the light within,
and shine,
forever certain.

You make me feel like
every imperfection has
been perfectly placed
to reflect beauty in
the mirror.

You make me feel like
the world has conspired
to bring us closer.

And in the end,
if it's only one thing
that really mattered,
it was that you
made me feel.

WRITTEN IN THE STARS

Like the stars that
came crashing together
in a force of nature
that gave birth to
the entire universe—
we came together.

The explosion that
started the beginning
of life as we know it
are the same sparks
that fly between us.

The light that illuminates
the entire world is
the sun radiating from
our connection.

But not like the Sun
of high noon.

It's more like the subtle
sunlight of sunrise—
easy on the eyes.

So healing that you can
stare at it without going
blind.

Now, that kind of light,
is hard to find.

SELFLESS

The fact is true love
is nurtured beyond
the point of self.

It puts you under a
magical spell.

Permitting you to bathe
in a compassionate well.

The water seeps
into your pores.

Every drop healing the
colorful open sores.

THE DEPTH OF NOW

Your presence
inspires me.

It reminds me
to sit quietly.

To observe the
space between
words and listen
to the stillness.

DIVINE LOVE

My love for you is pure.

As pure as honey straight
from the hive.

My love drips for you
covering everything
in its path.

PART OF ME

You are a part of me,
like my tear drops
singing songs of you,
you drip out of me,
painting the streets
with your love.

In every movement
of my lips,
I remember you.
Like the time
you whispered
in my ear
that I was the woman
of your dreams.

With every roll
of my tongue,
I speak you.
As if your words
are spilling out of me
when I say that
things will work out,
and the sanctity
of our love
is enough
to last through

The Journey: Night to Dawn

the scarcity
of our touch
caused by the long
droughts of distance.

For every touch
on the end of my
fingertips,
I feel you.
Like floating flowers,
we floated in space
between earth and dreams,
because neither seems
to be the right place for us.

You are a part of me,
and like the moon waiting
to catch a glimpse of
the sun as it rises,
I wait to catch a glimpse
of your heart unraveling.

UNBEARABLE

Hold my mouth
closed so
I can't whisper
this sorrow.

The cold skin
against my warm
ruby lips
doesn't soften
the blow.

The water flowing
from mouth to mouth,
like the sweet saliva
of a romantic kiss.

That must have
been the last one,
I thought to myself.

It will surely
be missed.

BREATHE

My heart hurts
from this obsession,
I can't get you
out of my head.

As I tried to fight,
the more I bled.

This bleeding that
never ceases,
flowing like a river
of pain across
the broken pieces.

The Journey: Night to Dawn

I wish I never
wanted you.

I wish I never
needed you.

My only sin
was wanting to
be with you.

LONGING

I sit next to
the windowsill
watching the
rain drops hang
on the glass.

So close,
yet so far
from falling.

Every moment
they grow
heavier,
like my heart
when it aches
for you.

Missing you
is like missing
the sun.

IMPERMANENCE

It's like the
universe
doesn't want us
to meet again.

It's as if that
one time eclipsed
in the symphony
of eternity,
was cut short
by our destiny
of being
temporary
lovers.

TRANSFORMATIVE

I need
wholehearted,
vulnerable love.

I need love that
isn't afraid to show
it's scars and
bloodied fists.

I need love that
whispers to the
demons—

that this is
the last time
they will suck
the blood of
my being.

REFLECTIONS

Was it I
who was in
the wrong?

Perhaps,
I was too
dependent.

Perhaps,
I lost myself
in the fervent
of my own
love.

Perhaps,
it wasn't his
responsibility
to mend
the hole
within me.

HOT POTATO LOVE

You never got
my whole heart
because you were
too afraid to
hold her in
your arms.

You were afraid
to open up
and accept
my vulnerability
for what she was,
so in playing
hot potato with
my beating organ
you dropped her
and made her still.

THE COLLAPSE

It was 30 days of
not seeing you
and I tried to
forget the
loneliness
that you left
with me.

To fill the
emptiness
inside of me
after you
left me
bare bones
on the vinyl
floor.

I tried to prop
myself up
on the shoulders
of other men
to keep me
from falling again,
but my wrists
gave way.

STUCK IN THE PAST

I used to think
that I was only
safe in your arms,
but that was just
an illusion.

One meant to
protect me,
but just kept
me stuck.

GRIEVING

Dark and alone,
my body implodes.

The wave of heaviness
consumes me.

I can't see or hear
overcome by
crippling fear.

My mind wanders
and it's quite somber.

Thoughts of all
the pain and suffering
in this world,
I feel it all.

It goes down
my veins like a
cascading waterfall.

Mind and spirit
unite in the mist,
realization that this
doesn't really exist.

Then relief settles in.

And in the end,
it's my belief
in the power
of grief
that will win.

DARK NIGHT OF THE SOUL

There may be moments in life where the rug is pulled out from underneath you. Where everything that you've been holding onto for your identity & security dissolves into thin air. Those moments are painful. Sometimes excruciating. But those are the same moments where great possibility is born. And if you answer the call, those could be the very moments where the greatest version of yourself comes into being.

THE LIES WE MUST UNLEARN

I am so
desperate
for love that
I would rather
mold and bend
myself into
smallness
instead of
face loneliness.

Because somehow
being loved in
my smallness
makes me worthy
of love.

That's

the biggest lie

I ever believed.

BECOMING

Maybe I needed
to wait this long
so that I could see
that the only person
I really needed
was me.

SALT

Tear drops,
tear spots,
falling down
my face.

The pace,
quicker
than ever.

The feeling,
forever lingering.

It's that tingling
that won't let
go from
the bottom of
my stomach
to the top of
my throat.

It feels like
I'm on a boat
floating in tears
washed up by fears,
of the unknown.

REPRESSED MEMORIES

There are gaps
in my memory.

Gaps that I
cannot see.

Even when it's
in front of me
acting like a sea
of experience,
coming with a wave
from the past.

It disappears on
the shores,
almost as quick
as I heard its roar.

THE MISSING LINK

The day I spoke
to my mother and
confronted her
with questions
trying to fill the
memories of my past
was a day I will
never forget.

I knew there
was something
missing from
my story.

It was that
inner sight
that something
wasn't right.

That it was
unconsciously
leading my life.

The words hit me
like a ton of bricks.

*You were 3 or 4
when you came home
from preschool with
bloody underwear.*

HIDDEN FLAME

I used to be
a tenacious
little girl.

One that was
full of will and
determination,
but I learned
at a young age
that it could
hurt me beyond
unimaginable
pain.

So I locked
it all away.

AVERSION

I've been running
from my problems
for so long,
I forgot which
problems
I'm running
from.

Maybe they're just
a figment of my
imagination,
likely just a
fabrication
of my
conditioning.

SURVIVAL INSTINCTS

The things
we do to
survive,
to protect
ourselves
and hide.

Sooner or
later become
poison to the mind.

Especially when
we have to lie.

To claim that
we must be
defective or else
these events
wouldn't occur.

They wouldn't
create such
a stir,
if only
we were
worthy
of love.

TRIAL AND ERROR

It's taken me years
to understand
what kind of love
I want.

Years of not
loving myself,
turned into decades
of putting myself in a
neatly wrapped box.

You see, that's what
I thought you wanted.

So, I hid and
made myself as
small as a peanut,
barely even visible.

BOUNDARIES

I didn't know
I was allowed
to have boundaries
until you crossed
them for the last
time.

CLOSED THROAT

I feel like
there's cotton
stuck down
my throat.

Every time I
try to speak
fear creeps in
for the kill.

If only the words
would shoot out
like rockets before
I had a chance
to imprison them
against their
will.

THE DANGERS
OF APPROVAL

I spent my whole
life trying to
please others—
to squeeze every
ounce of approval
for all it's worth.

I morphed and
bent like a pretzel
without any desire
to be Rapunzel.

I got locked away
in a tower.

No flowers,
no happily ever
after.

GROWING PAINS

Emotions rock
the ocean of
my insides and
I can't seem
to hide.

I left the bottle and
leaf behind.

Nothing now to
soothe the pain
except nature,
and my own
mind.

DISCONNECTED

We met when
I was a fetus
in the womb
of my mother.

After birth I had
to get used to you,
to know how
to use you.

To move through
you to get what
I needed to.

And it was you who
carried me through
all along.

You burdened the
weight of my wounds
over the years,
limping over
every now
and again out of
sheer exhaustion.

I've been neglecting
you body,
and I'm so sorry
I've ignored you
for so long.

I'm sorry I never
protected you,
cradled you
and held you
like you needed
me to.

You my body
have been
so good to me,
but I never
took the time
to know you.

ON THE CONDITIONING
OF MEN

A man who can't
cry tears is just
a hurting man
who's turned
to stone.

He feels all alone
as he's abandoned
his true self
in exchange for
counterfeit wealth
in the form of strength.

If only he knew that
even the softest water
can break through
the toughest of stone—
he would be free.

TOUGH LOVE

The saddest part about never
being able to talk to
my father about feelings
is that he's never been able
to acknowledge the full range
of his own.

GENERATIONAL TRAUMA

Trauma runs
in our family.

It's been
passed down
from generation
to generation.

And like hand me
down clothes,
we can never seem
to let it go.

LESSONS FOR MY DAUGHTER

Don't ever
allow a man
to control
any square inch
of your body.

Not even one.

Not even
the tip of your
pinky nail.

Because one
turns to two
turns to three
and four and
before you know it,
your body is
no longer yours.

NOT ALL GOOD IS CREATED EQUAL

The virus that
every culture
plants in the minds
of little girls—
being a *good*
girl.

The amount of
agony I've seen
painted on young
girls' faces
as they strive
for this illusionary
goodness.

The voices that have
been tamed and quieted,
who say yes,
when they mean
no.

Who say thank you,
when they mean
never again.

That's the kind
of good
that kills
souls.

INVISIBLE VEIL

Abuse doesn't have
to show up with
marks.

Often times its
hidden in the
dark.

In the slur of the
words used to hurt.

Used to cut you
down like an
axe to a pine
tree.

Who would even
understand the
insidiousness of
the letters strung
together and
slung across the
kitchen table?

Only the abused—
and the abuser.

GOLDEN CAGE

Like birds with
clipped wings,
their belief that
they could fly
was denied at
a young age.

So they stayed
in the bird house,
where they thought
they were safe.

They didn't know that
the house kept them
caged.

PASSING DOWN DARKNESS

One of the saddest things
that broken couples do
is to have children so that
they can pull through
the darkness that has
ensued their union.

What they don't realize
is that they place the
burden of the dark
on the child
and it's first years
are spent trying to
climb out of the
shadows.

Some,
never make it.

PUSH-PULL

Many of us
are led by
our wounds.

We're either
attracted or
repulsed
because of
our past.

If we don't
heal fast,
it will control
our lives
and we
will call
it destiny.

THE FIXER

The truth is
you can't heal
what you can't
see.

And in your
blindness
it's easy to focus
on your sweet
pea.

But that's just a
masterful illusion
created by fear.

Refusing to let
you hear
the cries from
the universe,
that it's you
who's hurt.

HEALING WOUNDS

Yesterday I couldn't
take one step
without rivers
flowing from my
eyes.

Some days
I can't seem to
shake the pain
so I just let the
tears neutralize.

I wring them
out in the streets
or in between
my sheets
as an offering
to the skies.

PERSPECTIVE

You can label
an event as
terrifying or freeing
based on your
perspective.

The same event
can trigger all
of your fears
and shake you
to your core

Or it can
liberate you
like never
before.

99 PROBLEMS

I am only
as big as
you make me.

Sincerely,
Your problems

SURRENDERING

Be honest with
yourself.

Be unapologetically you
even if they don't
want you to.

Ascend to the skies
with your eyes on
the prize.

Evolve chapter after
chapter in your book
and write your
story with failures,
tragedies and all.

Don't let them
scare you out
of the fall.

RADICAL ACCEPTANCE

This face has seen
half the world with
its eyes
and yet there
still lies
the unknown
in this body
of mine

On the 30th day
of my 30th year
I stand before you here
in front of the mirror,
bare.

I see my reflection
and recognize this body
as my own,
but as a look closer
my eyes and chest
have grown.

My heart has
expanded to the
size of my face
and I will no longer
be disgraced by
my own vulnerability

or who I *seem* to be
to the girl in the mirror.

You see I'm
an unwavering being
with a deep-rooted soul
that sits among Goddesses.

And the truth is
I won't let anyone
tell me otherwise,
not even you
in the mirror.

So I'm letting
you go…

TO MY ANCESTORS

For my female ancestors
who felt helpless
at every turn,
I am here.

I am here
to break the
generational patterns
of disappointment
when the clan refused
to accept her
totally.

I am here to push
the boundaries of what
it means to be
fully free in this
feminine body.

I am here to bury
the sadness and grief
once and for all.

THINGS I WISH YOU KNEW

What if you walked around like you were deeply loved? What if you moved through the world like the universe and everyone in your life was holding you with their Love. What if you knew that Love is carrying you through your joys, and your sadness?

THE CHALLNEGE
OF SELF-LOVE

I've never known a love
like this from another,
except from my mother.

But I began to give myself
this nurturing love.

I stumbled along the way,
always in dismay,
at how difficult this was.

THE ROAD TO WHOLENESS

The path to healing
is not what you
may imagine.

It's not linear
nor logical.

You might achieve
a huge milestone
only to be met
with more
sadness.

UNPREDICTABLE

Some nights I
feel alone in
this world
struggling to
heal myself.

And other nights
I'm in the company
of the entire universe
vibrating within
my veins.

ONLY YOU

In healing
you have to
keep reminding
yourself that
you don't need
anyone's approval
to heal.

Repeat after me:
"the only person
that I need to heal
is my whole self and
nobody else."

CLEANSING

Today, the rains cleansed
my soul of the pain.

As I stood in between
mother earth and father sky,
it just all went away.

SHADOWS

The parts of
my mind
are like the
colors of the
rainbow splattered
onto a palette.

Some are bright
and bold,
others are dark
and dull,
but they all
come together
to paint a
beautiful
picture.

With the same breath
I speak my deepest
fear & desire:

to be seen.

A NEW WAY

Old things bubble up
and they put on such
a fuss.

Letting go
is not enough.

I have to chop them
to pieces,
dissect them
and fertilize them
with feces.

That's the only way
I can move beyond
the past.

To treat the soil
with lessons of turmoil
while planting seeds
for tomorrow.

THE JOURNEY

This journey is not
for the lighthearted.

It's not for those
who get nauseous
at the sight of blood—
for a lot of blood will be
spilled along the way.

The wounds that
have been festering
split open by the
pressure of time.

That's when the
real healing
begins.

THE SHEDDING

It was the
last night of
my old life.

The very last drop
of what was,
dripped out of
me.

All the pain
of the past,
no longer had
a home within
my body.

BREAKING OPEN

Through all the pain,
all the cracks in my skin,
I can now see clearly.

I can see my light
illuminating as bright
as the sun.

The brightness was
always there,
I just never
broke myself open
in this way.

HOW TO BE ACCEPTED

In order for others
to accept you—
you need to accept
the dark & neglected
parts of yourself.

The parts that
you show to
no one else.

These are the parts
that need the most
help.

They need the
nurturing love
that comes from
the eternal one.

The subliminal
spirit.

Can you hear it?

As it whispers
in your ear,
everything that
you've been
wanting to hear.

That you are loved.

SELF MASTERY

Sometimes life
teaches you lessons
in the form of
mirrors.

Your external experiences
are just a reflection
of what's going on
inside.

The law of attraction
from the subconscious
mind.

She will keep teaching
you those lessons
until one day,
you become
the master.

HONORING MOTHER

What if to move forward
we first need to go back.

Back to the very beginning.

To that moment when god made
Eve out of Adam's rib,
but instead of making her
from a part of him,
using the same
exact formula.

The divine combination
of god and earth.

I wonder then if there
would be a new birth.

A rebirth of our philosophy,
of what it means to be
womanly.

I AM WOMAN

People look at me
as if I am weak,
but they know
not of my peak.

They know nothing
of my capabilities
or the so-called truth
that they seek.

They only see what
they want to believe,
but they know not
of the real me.

I am a woman.

I am a mother
awaiting birth.

I am a human
being.

I am everything in
between the sun
and moon.

I am as powerful
as a pacific typhoon.

I am.

THE SELF

It may seem as
if I'm endlessly
searching the planet
for the magic,
but I've already
found it.

I already know
of its existence
and whereabouts.

The question is
when will I uncover
the doubts.

When will I discard
the mask and reveal
the truth.

I might just need
a little boost,
a nudge from
the universe or perhaps
the experience to
unearth.

To unearth this
wonderful, ethereal
element of life.

I bet it's been
there all along,

as quiet as the night.

And by the end,
I think I might just
have it right.

It's me.

I am the one who
I endlessly seek.

The inner being with
a gentle mystique.

Don't you forget to
climb to the peak.

And there you will find
eternal love so to speak.

MY DEFINITION OF FREEDOM

Freedom is relinquishing
the chains of self-doubt.

Freedom is the expression
of love in the depths of sorrow.

Freedom is the choice
to live honestly, unaffected
by the confinement
of social norms.

Freedom is earth and water
flowing down a mountainside
flooding into the ocean.

Freedom is humanity fighting
for the rights of all.

Freedom is loving yourself
despite the imperfections.

Freedom to live,
Freedom to love,
Freedom to be.

Freedom to imagine
a world without hate—
instead one that
is fueled by love.

Unconditional,
selfless,
beautiful love.

The kind of love that
only lovers know of.

The kind of love that goes
from Me to I to You to We,
and then back to You again.

It's You.

It's *all* You.

You are the creator
of this realm.

You give birth
to Freedom.

You are the one
who can make
the choice.

You are Love.

You should find
the time
to unwind.

My mother's smile
could start & end wars
in one sweep.

RADIANT

My beauty is not defined
by the symmetry of my face
nor the blackened tops of
my eyelids.

It is not defined
by the simple curves
of my body
or the flatness of my
belly.

My beauty is defined
by the way my lips
quiver when I speak truth
for the first time
unsure of its reception.

It is defined by
my heart which is still
tender from the struggles
of my past.

It's defined by my inner
search for the beauty within
because that
is the only beauty
that I want to
define me.

DEATH/REBIRTH

We go through many
little deaths in
a lifetime,
some bigger than
we like.

But there's
always that one
that changes
the course of
your life.

DEEP

You deserve to
have pleasure.

You are worthy
of a love so deep
that even the ocean
would envy its depth.

IF I HAD A CHILD

If I had a child,
I would show it the
spectacular beauty
in everyday flaws
because its flaws that
make us who we are
and imperfection is the
greatest gift of all.

I would teach it that
heartbreak is nothing more
than getting to know your
true self in another's
reflection.

That love
is an eternal expression,
and may fade away with time,
but will never die.

MESSAGES

Take this as a sign
that you can find
the strength within you
to build castles & empires
with the threads of
your dreams.

LESSONS FROM THE OCEAN

The ocean
teaches me
to be soft yet
powerful.

To be vast in
stillness yet
have the power
to move forward.

The ocean she
always shows
me love.

It's as if the whole
world is saying
You are welcome here
when I arrive at
her door.

PROTECT YOUR ENERGY

Don't let anyone
heedlessly feed
off your energy.

For energy is meant
to be mutually shared
not devoured.

And what most surely
accompanies a devouring
is death.

INTUITION

I learned the hard way
that the demons within
create the monsters
outside.

And the only way
to defeat them
is to see without
your eyes.

WARRIOR WOMEN

You are more brave
than you ever
thought possible.

Your existence despite
the dark clouds that
chased you down
proves that.

You come from a long
lineage of brave women
who survived through famines
& wars & unimaginable
pain—
just so they could
have you.

Bravery
is in your
blood.

To those
who have
experienced
heart wrenching
heartbreak,
and heartache.
Know one thing—
you have lived.

HOW TO RECONCILE
YOUR PAST

Every time you think
that thought,
just close your eyes
and breath.

Inhale the oxygen
from the trees.

Fill your lungs
to full capacity
and repeat after
me.

I am so much more
than a collection of
my sorrows.

And everything
I fear is already
gone but I am
here in the present.

I am that bioluminescent
light that shines bright,
forever in the eternal
presence.

HONORING SELF

The more we hide who we truly are—our true feelings, needs and desires—the more we seek for others to fill this gaping hole within us. Even though most of us don't share these aspects of ourselves due to fear of rejection, what we're really doing is rejecting ourselves. Make sure that in the game of life you don't end up betraying the one person who has been there through it all—you.

COMING HOME

There are times
that you will find
yourself alone
in your own
company.

Cherish those
moments.

Honor them for
what they truly are.

You,
with the love
of your life.

ROOTS

Every touch of
my bare feet on
the soil brings my
breath to life.

Every view of
the plains bowing
down to the sun
makes my heart
skip a beat.

A beat like the
cow-skinned drums
thumping with the
sound of celebration.

A beat like the
movement of my hips
swaying with seduction.

A beat like I will never
have to fear the day
for I have already
lived.

I have lived moments
and years on
faraway lands
and that is enough
to bring my memory
back to my roots.

YOUR GIFT

Don't waste
your privilege
on doing
something
that sucks
the soul
dry.

SELF EXPRESSION

I express myself
for the women
in my lineage
who couldn't.

I dance for
the women
who still to
this day are
forced to stop
the joyous
movement of
bodies in song.

I honor myself
so that those
who come
after me
may know
that they are
worthy of
honor.

Your heart
is special,
honor it.

HOW-TO

How to feel
vibrant, internally
and externally.

Step 1: love
yourself unconditionally.

Step 2: Nourish your
body and mind equally.

Step 3: Surrender selflessly
to the unfolding of life.

FREE WOMAN

This life is
not meant
to be lived
hidden in the
shadows.

Too many of
my sisters have
been stripped of
their freedom for
me to squander
mine on what
other people
think.

FREEDOM FROM BEING YOU

You are more than just your mind or your body.
There is a place within you that is as expansive
as the ocean and as eternal as undying love.

WHISPERS

Have you ever
quieted yourself
so that you could
feel the warm embrace
of your soul speaking
without words?

EARS OF THE HEART

Life is guiding
us whether we
like it or not.

With every moment,
you can choose to
see with your eyes
or listen with your
heart.

SACRED LIFE

Every moment,
an encounter
with that which
moves us.

This is how life
is supposed to
be.

NATURE'S WAY

Just as a tree
twists and turns
to touch the sun,
you too shall touch
the soul.

THE ETERNAL

Light flickers
behind my
closed eyes.

Does it come
from within or
from the outside?

Something tells me
it's the light
that never dies.

THE WATER

Have you ever
listened to the
water?

Sat close enough
to hear its voice
whisper to you?

Your mind may
not comprehend it
but your heart
knows that the
vibrations are
more than just
ripples in the water

They are an ocean
of words speaking
the song of your
soul.

THE FIRE

There's only one
life to live,
the one of
your deepest
desires.

Nowhere else
will you find
the eternal
fire.

SWEET LEAF

That sweet leaf
got me swimming
in a reef
full of coral
and colors
way down under.

Under the depth
of my soul
so that I
might know
what it's like
to touch God.

To connect with
the universe
in such a way
that it doesn't all
seem to slip away
between my fingertips.

Because somehow
you can still grasp
the sunlight
in your hands.

You can still
touch the earth
with your feet.

You see it reminds me
that you don't have to
lose your sight to live.

That you can be
in tune with the moon
waxing and waning
with the tides.

Just in it for
the ride.

PURPOSE

I'm here to learn
about the parts of
myself that I've
forgotten.

The part that
exudes joy and
ecstasy.

The part that
needs just the earth,
water and wind
for a content life.

I'm here to learn
about the fire inside
that burns bright.

And like the sun,
the part that fights
the night with
pure light.

And then, the trees
and the moon
whispered to her,
we are the same.

STROKES

Life is a
creative dance
of nature so
why not create
worlds with
every breath &
universes with
every stroke?

THE FEMININE

And then,
she worked
tirelessly
to leave
the world
more beautiful
then it was when
she arrived.

The Journey: Night to Dawn

ABOUT THE AUTHOR

Laila Sahar Jewayni is a writer, creative, and holistic wellness practitioner. She started avidly writing at 23 when she found that expressing her feelings through poetry came naturally to her—she hasn't stopped writing since. Now, 34, her work is focused on helping others heal through coming back to their innate wisdom. Her poetry reflects her own healing journey embracing the hard and messy parts, as well as the glorious parts, of being human.

44276224R00069